THE ALL-NEW KIDS' STUFF BOOK OF CREATIVE MATH EXPERIENCES FOR THE YOUNG CHILD

by Imogene Forte and Joy MacKenzie

Incentive Publications, Inc.
Nashville, Tennessee

Illustrated by Gayle Harvey
Cover by Marta Drayton
Edited by Jennifer J. Streams and Angela L. Reiner

ISBN 0-86530-476-9

Copyright ©2001 by Incentive Publications, Inc., Nashville, TN. All rights reserved. No part of this publication may be reproduced, stored in a retrieval system, or transmitted in any form or by any means (electronic, mechanical, photocopying, recording, or otherwise) without written permission from Incentive Publications, Inc., with the exception below.

Pages labeled with the statement ©**2001 by Incentive Publications, Inc., Nashville, TN** are intended for reproduction. Permission is hereby granted to the purchaser of one copy of **THE ALL-NEW KIDS' STUFF BOOK OF CREATIVE MATH EXPERIENCES FOR THE YOUNG CHILD** to reproduce these pages in sufficient quantities for meeting the purchaser's own classroom needs only.

PRINTED IN THE UNITED STATES OF AMERICA
www.incentivepublications.com

Table of Contents

How to Use This Book 7

Learning About Shapes 9
- Circles 10
- Add Some Circles 11
- Squares 12
- Find the Squares 13
- Color the Squares 14
- Rectangles 15
- Triangles 16
- Great Taste in Shapes 17
- Shape Review 18

Learning to Read and Write Numbers 19
- One 20
- Two 22
- Three 24
- Four 26
- Five 28
- Six 30
- Seven 32
- Eight 34
- Nine 36
- Ten 38
- A Story About Zero 40
- Dot-to-Dot 41
- Numerals to Color 42
- Find the Number 44
- Fish 'n' Fun 45
- Chicken Coop 46
- Cock-A-Doodle-Do 47
- Shutdown for Robot Repair! 48
- Who's in the Barnyard? 49
- Climb the Tipsy Tower! 50
- Number Puzzles 51
- Picture Talk 52
- Make Your Own Book 53
- Numeral Review 55
- Number Word Review 56

Counting by Sets 57
- Sets 58
- Sweet Sets 59
- Who's Hiding Under the Steps? 60
- Draw the Sets 61
- Show How Many 62
- Spider Sets 63
- Pairs 64
- Sets of Pairs 65
- Bee Busy! 66
- Boxes 'n' Bows 67
- Dinner's On! 68
- Creature Feature 69
- Set – Match 70

Using Size Words 71
   Big 72
   Large 73
   Little 74
   Small 75
   Which is Which? 76
   Faces 77
   Small Creatures 78
   Circle and Color 79
   Long and Short 80
   The Long and Short of It 81
   Long, Longer, Longest 82
   Tall, Taller, Tallest 83
   Mark the Road 84
   Fewer or More 85
   Size Words Review 86

Living with Numbers 87
   Numbers... Numbers... Everywhere 88
   Special Numbers 89
   Telephone Time 90
   Numbers with Buying Power 91
   Dollar Bills 92
   Toy Store 93
   Price Tags 94
   Count and Rhyme 95
   Numbers to Count Down! 96
   The Race is On 97
   Numbers to Grow On 98
   Weigh Up 99

   More Numbers to Grow On 100
   Numbers for Travel 102
   Mark the Trail 103
   Numbers to Celebrate 104
   Happy Birthday 105
   Numbers to Get Up and Go By 106
   What Time Is It? 107
   This is Buzzy 108
   Numbers for Finding Things 109
   Numbers to Order and Eat 110
   Calorie Counting 111
   Measuring Cups 112
   Measuring Up 113
   Whole and Half 114
   Two Halves = One Whole 115
   Half or Whole 117
   Hot and Cold 118
   Check the Temperature 119
   Numbers on the Computer 120

Test Yourself 121
   X Marks the Answer 121
   Circle the Set 122
   Which is Which? 123
   Living with Numbers Review 124

Vocabulary for Math 125

HOW TO USE THIS BOOK

Instructions for Parents and Teachers

Many creative teachers have found that children can deal effectively with mathematical concepts at an earlier age than has been previously thought. The child's environment should be saturated with opportunities to use numbers in natural and meaningful settings. As children are guided in counting objects and people; in learning the use of numerals on clocks, calendars, measuring cups, rulers, and scales; and in observing the variations and relationships in sizes and shapes of objects, they are building beginning math concepts.

The mastery of these all-important foundational concepts and understandings is developmental in nature and should be presented in proper sequence with their readiness based on past experiences and present interests. This phase of the young child's intellectual development should be planned and carefully monitored by an adult who is sensitive to the rate of progress being made and to the need for redirection or reinforcement in specific areas. It is important to remember that learning is continuous and developmental, and that each stage of mathematical growth is dependent upon success in the stage that preceded it. The activities in *Creative Math Experiences for the Young Child* are sequentially planned and should be introduced to the child as they are presented in the book.

To provide help in determining when a child has mastered the basic concepts, skills, and factual information related to each of the five areas presented, a review is included at the end of each section. The review should be administered and scored with adult guidance, and immediate feedback should be furnished to the child.

Learning About Shapes

As young children are exposed to different shapes, they learn to recognize the shapes and to identify them in their natural environment. Transfer of this awareness to patterns in sidewalks, clothing, kites, buildings, and other everyday objects heightens sensitivity to the world. As they add the words *triangle*, *rectangle*, *square*, and *circle* to their vocabularies, important concepts related to skill development in both language and math are being established. Matching, copying, and reproducing these shapes helps the child acquire the all-important visual discrimination skills that are prerequisite to reading readiness.

Each of the activities in this section is designed to help children fulfill these basic developmental needs. Adult guidance in completing the activities should be consistently patient yet firm, and should be adjusted to the child's natural rate of progress.

Learning to Read and Write Numbers

Counting by rote is often mistaken as evidence of a child's understanding of the counting process or of readiness to work with abstract number concepts. Real objects that can be touched as they are counted should be included as a regular part of early counting experiences. Use of rhyming words, finger plays, and games will also enrich and strengthen understanding. These activities have been planted to give experience in meaningful counting and to extend concepts to include use of printed symbols and related vocabulary.

Counting by Sets

Children need to understand that sets are simply groups or collections of objects. Grouping things into sets and discovering how sets may be manipulated develop concepts of union and subsets. It is through counting objects in various sets that the cardinal meaning of numerals can be developed. *More than, less than, smaller than, larger than,* and other mathematical relationships become well understood and useful additions to the child's store of intellectual assets.

Using Size Words

Remembering the importance of concrete experiences to the attainment of meaningful concepts, size words, and other vocabulary extensions must be planned as an integral part of the sequentially developed math program. Understanding and use of these words enhance the quest for in-depth and more abstract learning. Their presentation will provide the base for the emergence of number language in the most meaningful sense. Completion of these exercises with adult guidance adjusted to the child's individual needs should provide the reinforcement necessary to solidify understanding of size words and their application to problem-solving situations.

Living with Numbers

Learning about numbers is hardly worthwhile if there is no application to real-life situations. Is the child aware of the use of numbers as they appear in elevators, on T.V. and computer screens, menus, telephones, mailboxes, license plates, and addresses?

In assessing individual readiness for the development of concepts of measurement, it is important to listen to the child talk to determine if his/her vocabulary includes words related to shape, size, amount, capacity, time, and distance. The child whose attention has been called to the clock and the calendar as important tools for social living, to the thermometer and scales as useful for gaining desirable information, and to measuring cups and spoons as indispensable in the kitchen is much more apt to approach the exercises in this section with zeal and commitment.

The young child's introduction to fractions should be limited to basic beginning concepts and in most cases should not be extended beyond the whole and half stage. Simple use of parts of a whole and the acquisition of related vocabulary is the chief concern of the activities in this section. Verbalization of terms such as *both, divide, double, middle, alike,* and *two parts* is desirable as the activities are being completed. Reinforcement can also be afforded through directions such as "fold your sheet of paper in the middle and use only one half of it for your picture" or "divide the stack of pennies in half."

Today's children are naturally curious about and interested in money. They know from an early age that certain objects can be had or not had because of money. Discussion of cost of toys or sweets, and money in the piggy bank, trips to the store, and opportunities to spend small amounts of money will give meaning to developing concepts related to money.
The Vocabulary List (pgs. 125-127) is composed of words children need to know in order to begin developing math skills and concept mastery. It is suggested that they be cut apart, pasted on tag board or index cards, and laminated if possible; to be used for flash cards, games and word walls, as well as for drill and reinforcement.

There is no substitute for many and varied real-life experiences planned to be developmental in nature. For most children, the activities in *Creative Math Experiences for the Young Child* will be motivational in nature, and should be solidly reinforced by extensive discussion, trips, games, and manipulative experiences.

Learning About Shapes

Circles

Lines that are round in shape are called circles.

This shape is a circle.

Count the circles.

How many circles can you find in the picture? _____

Use a green crayon to circle each circle.

Name_____

Add Some Circles

Finish these pictures by adding some circles.

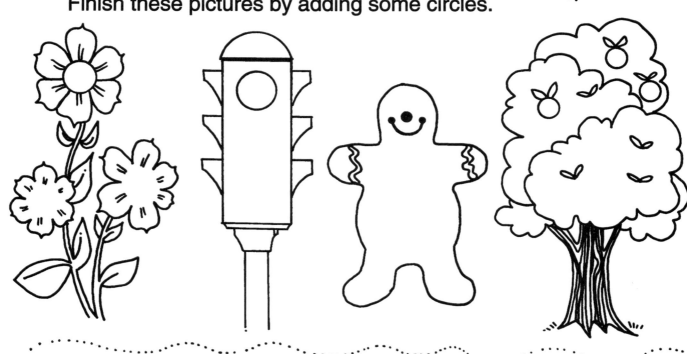

Use each group of circles to make a picture of your own.

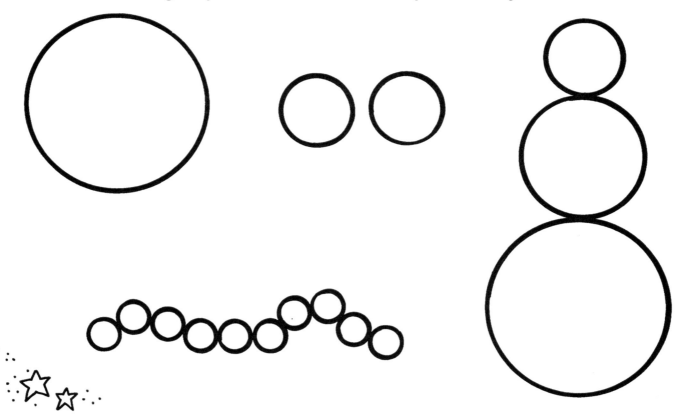

Name_____

Squares

This shape is a square.

How many sides does it have? ___

How many corners does it have? ___

If you said four, you are exactly right.

The sides of a square are all the same length.
All of its corners are the same.

Trace the squares with your finger.
Color each square orange.

Name_____

Find the Squares

Can you find the square shapes in the pictures below?

Trace them with your finger.

How many did you find? ___

Color the pictures you like best.

Name_____

Color the Squares

Find the squares in this design.

Color them red.

Color the other shapes green, yellow, or blue.

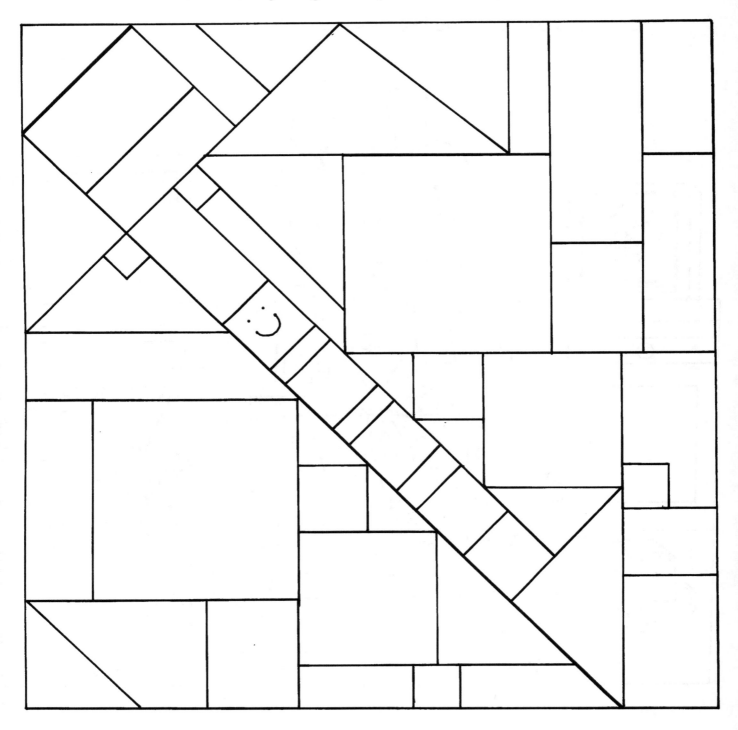

Name_____

Rectangles

Do you know what these shapes are called?

They are rectangles.

That's a big word. Say it three times.

>Rectangle!

>>Rectangle!

>>>Rectangle!

Rectangles have corners like squares, but their sides are not always the same length.

Only the sides that are opposite each other are the same length.

Color the rectangles.

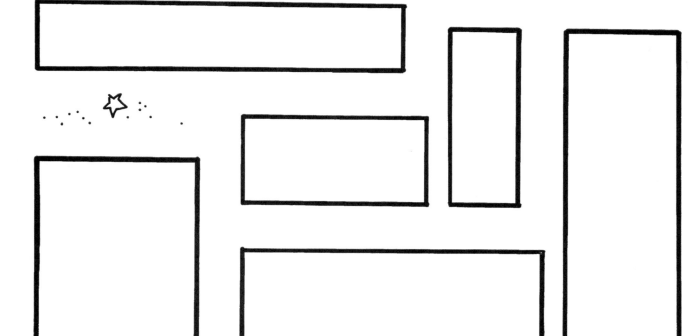

Name_____

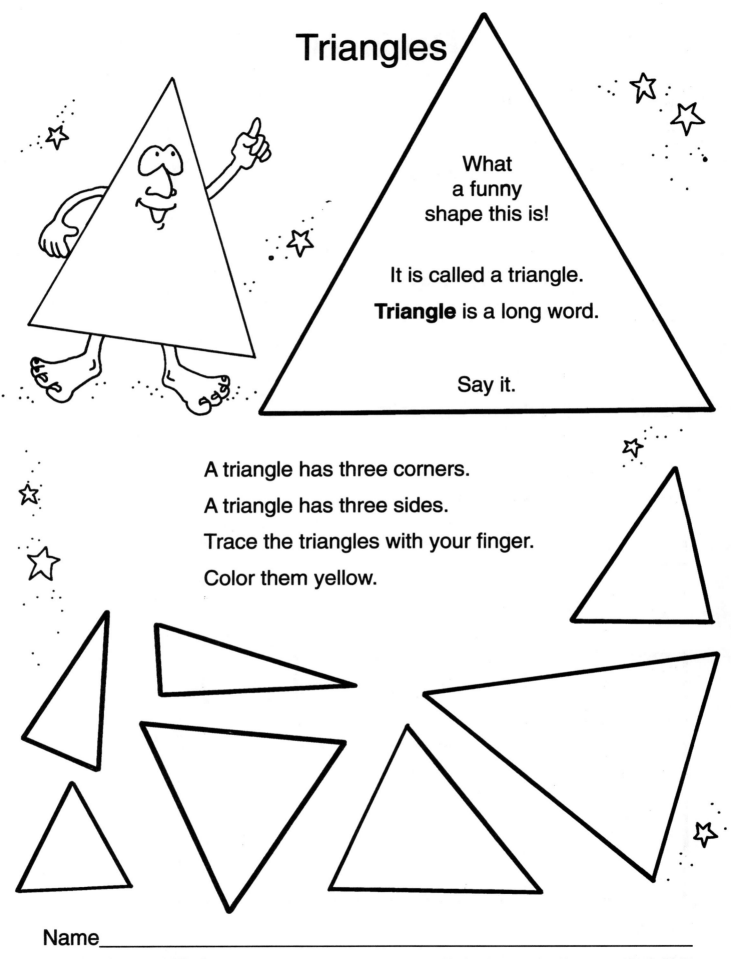

Great Taste in Shapes

To do this page, you will need a small cup of dry circle-shaped cereal.

Use your cereal to make this shape.
Circle its name.

triangle
circle
rectangle

Now make this shape.
Circle its name.

square
circle
rectangle

Can you make this shape?
Circle its name.

square
circle
triangle

Circle the name of this shape.
Make it with your cereal.

square
circle
rectangle

Eat the shapes in this order: □ △ ○ ▭

Name_____

Shape Review

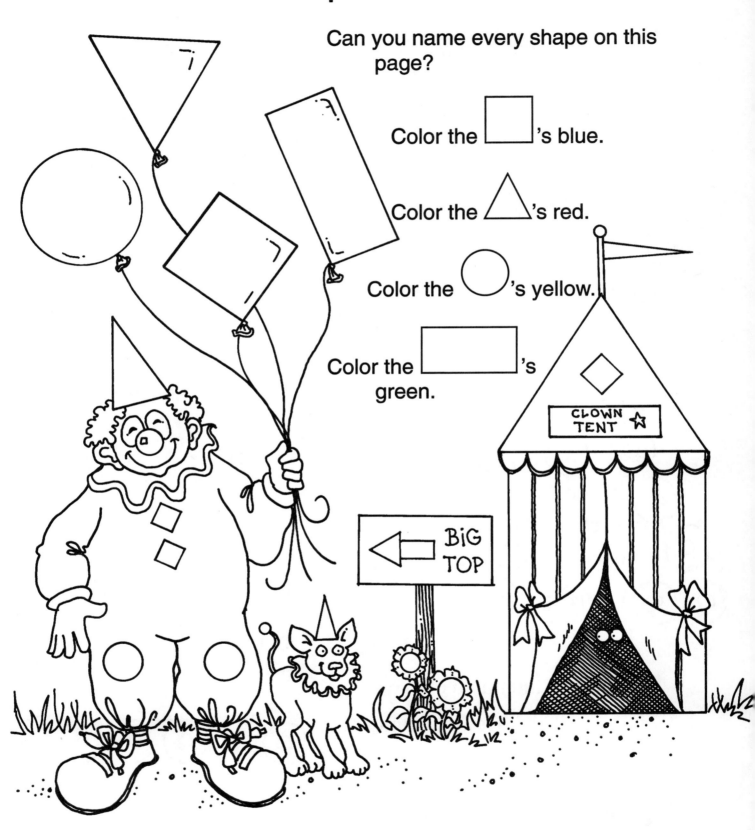

Can you name every shape on this page?

Color the ☐'s blue.

Color the △'s red.

Color the ○'s yellow.

Color the ▭'s green.

Name_____

Learning to Read and Write Numbers

One

1

How many hats are in this picture?

Color the picture pretty colors.

Practice writing the numeral.

_____

- -

_____

Name_____

One little girl is playing piñata.

Write the number word.

one

Name_____

2 Two

How many scarecrows are here?

Color the scarecrows.

Practice writing the numeral.

Name_____

Count the jack-o'-lanterns.

How many are happy?

Write the number word.

two

Name_____

Three

3

How many mice are here?

Color one mouse yellow.

Color two mice brown.

Practice writing the numeral.

_____

- -

_____

Name_____

How many cakes are here?

Color the cake that the mice have been eating.

Write the number word. three

Name_____

4 Four

How many turtles are here?

Color the turtles' hats.

Practice writing the numeral.

_____

- -

_____

Name_____

All-New Creative Math Experiences Copyright ©2001 by Incentive Publications, Inc., Nashville, TN.

Count the rabbits.

They are racing with the turtles.

Which do you think will win?

Pick a winner and color it gray.

Color the others green.

Write the number word.

four

Name_____

Five

5

Color the frogs.

Use your red crayon to color a tie on the one who is singing.

Practice writing the numeral.

_____

- -

_____

Name_____

Count the leaves.

Color one leaf red.

Color two leaves brown.

Color two leaves yellow.

How many leaves are there?

Write the number. _____

Write the number word.

Name_____

Six

How many mailboxes are here?

Use different crayons to color the mailboxes.

Practice writing the numeral.

Name_____

How many letters are here?

Color one letter yellow.

Color two letters blue.

Color three letters red.

Draw six letters in the mailbag.

Write the number word.

_____

- -

_____

Name_____

7 Seven

How many apple trees are in the picture?
Count and color them.

Practice writing the numeral.

Name_____

All-New Creative Math Experiences

Count the baskets.

Put an apple in each basket.

Count the apples.

Write the number word.

_____

- -

_____

Name_____

8 Eight

How many flowers are here?

Color the flowers many beautiful colors.

Practice writing the numeral.

_____

- - - - - - - - - - - - - - - - - - - -

_____

Name_____

Count the sprinkling cans.

Number them.

Write the number word.

_____

- -

_____

Name_____

Nine

9

How many bears are here?

Count and color them.

Make a yellow chin on the bear who has been licking the honey pot.

Practice writing the numeral.

_____

- -

_____

Name_____

All-New Creative Math Experiences

How many honeybees are here?

Color the bees yellow.

Write the number word.

Ten

How many parts does this train have?

Color the cars.

Count them.

Practice writing the numeral.

Name_____

Write the numerals 1-10 in the windows of this station house.

Write the number word.

ten

Name_____

A Story About Zero

0

This number is zero.

Zero means having none.

Make a zero in this box.

Betty had two kites.

The wind blew both of them away.

Now Betty has no kites at all. She has none.

Make a zero to tell how many kites Betty has.

Name_____

Dot-to-Dot

Follow the dots.
Color the picture.

Name_____

Numerals to Color

Color the numeral 1 red.
Color the numeral 2 blue.
Color the numeral 3 orange.
Color the numeral 4 yellow.
Color the numeral 5 green.

Name_____

Color the numeral 6 yellow.
Color the numeral 7 green.
Color the numeral 8 red.
Color the numeral 9 blue.
Color the numeral 10 orange.

Name_____

Find the Number

Underline the number word that is correct for each numeral. Color the numerals.

Fish 'n' Fun

Trace the number.

Then use your orange crayon to color that number of fish in each bowl.

Write the number word.

Name_____

Chicken Coop

Read the numeral on each nest.

Draw that many eggs in the nest.

3

5

4

Name_____

Cock-A-Doodle-Do

Follow the dots.

Color the picture red, orange, and yellow.

Name_____

Shutdown for Robot Repair!

The robot's keyboard has self-destructed.

Help repair it by writing the missing numerals.

Name_____

Who's in the Barnyard?

Count to find out how many of each animal is in the barnyard.

Write the correct numeral in each box.

Climb the Tipsy Tower!

Number the parts of the tipsy tower from bottom to top.

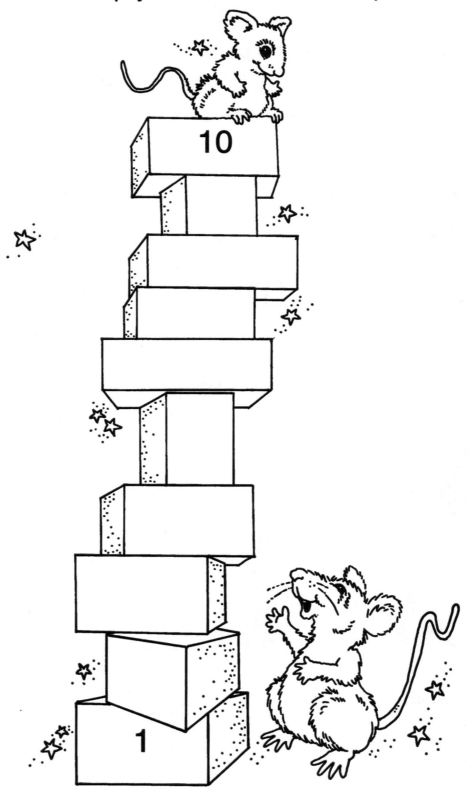

Name_____

Number Puzzles

Finish the crossword puzzles by completing the number words.

Words to Use

one	six
two	seven
three	eight
four	nine
five	ten

Picture Talk

Add hats to make this picture show six.

Make this picture show four trucks.

Put an X on the ones you do not need.

Make this picture show two cats.

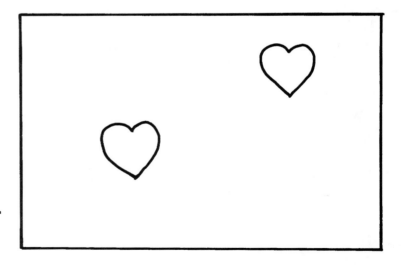

Make this picture show five hearts.

Make Your Own Book

Cut on the solid lines.

Fold on the dotted lines.

Name_____

Make Your Own Book (cont.)

Use your crayons to make each page of your book beautiful.

Name_____

Numeral Review

Write the numerals to show how many.

Number Word Review

Write each number word.

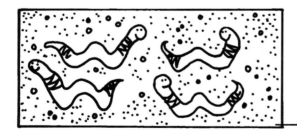

Name_____

Counting By Sets

Sets

A set is a group of things that are alike and together.

This is a set of three owls.

How many owls are in the set?

Write the numeral.

_____

This is a set of two umbrellas.

How many umbrellas are in the set?

Write the numeral.

_____

How many teapots are in this set?

Count them.

Write the numeral.

_____

Name_____

Sweet Sets

Each group of sweets is called a set of sweets.

How many? _____

How many? _____

How many? _____

How many? _____

How many different sets did you find? _____

Name_____

Who's Hiding Under the Steps?

Circle the correct picture to tell who's hiding where.

Who's hiding under a set of 3 steps?

Who's hiding under a set of 4 steps?

Who's hiding under a set of 2 steps?

Who's hiding under a set of 5 steps?

Name_____

Draw the Sets

Read each number below.

Write the correct numeral in each square.

Then draw a set to match that numeral in the rectangle.

Two — 2

Four

Six

Three

Five

Name_____

Show How Many

How many are in each set?

Write the numeral.

Name_____

Spider Sets

Color the set of two spiders green.

Color the set of four spiders orange.

Color the set of three spiders blue.

Name_____

Pairs

This is one shoe.

This is one pair of shoes.

A pair is a set of two things that go together.

Draw one shoe for a giant.

Draw a pair of mittens.

Draw a pair of socks.

Can you think of other things that come in pairs?

Name_____

Sets of Pairs

Match each numeral with a set of pairs.

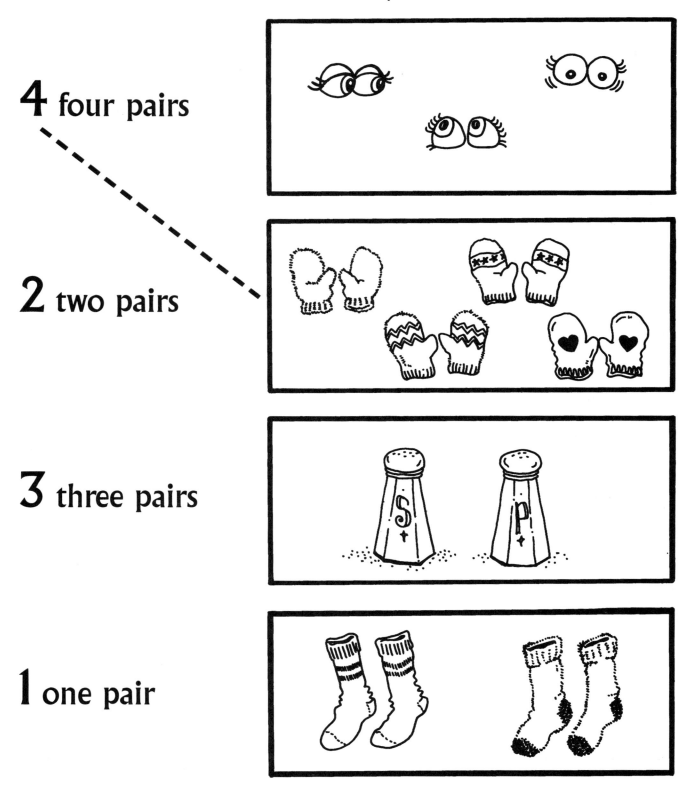

4 four pairs

2 two pairs

3 three pairs

1 one pair

Name_____

Bee Busy!

Draw a set of bees in each hive to match the set in each connecting hive.

Name_____

Boxes 'n' Bows

If the set on each package matches the number word below it, put a bow on the package.

If it does not match, put an X on the package.

four

five

six

eight

seven

three

Name_____

Dinner's On!

To do this page, you can use ten real pieces of corn or cereal, or you can draw the pieces.

Feed the puppy a set of two pieces.

Feed the chick a set of four pieces.

Feed the pig all the rest.

How many pieces did the pig get? _____

Name_____

Creature Feature

Complete the creature by drawing these sets on its body.

A set of two ears

A set of six hairs

A set of five teeth

A pair of hands

One big nose

Name_____

Set – Match

Color matching sets the same color:

Sets of four – yellow   Sets of three – green

Sets of five – blue   Sets of two – red

Name_____

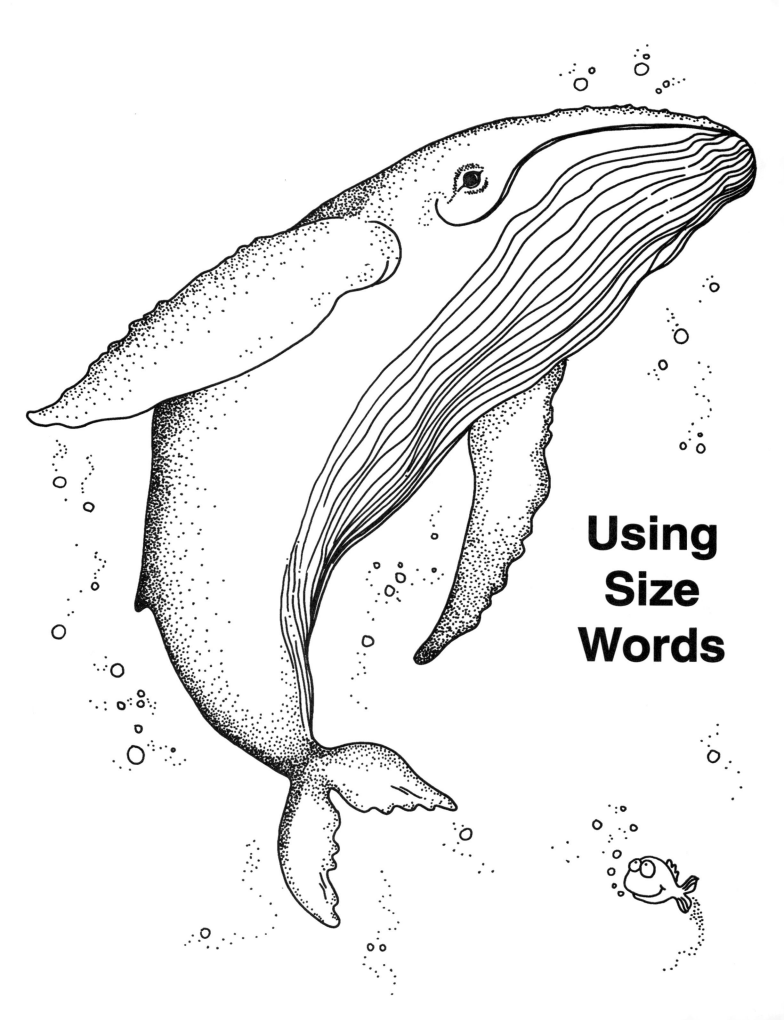

Using Size Words

Big

These are pictures of big things.

Another word for big is <u>large</u>.

Color the big tree green.

Color the large bear brown.

Color the big airplane blue.

Color the large barn red.

Name_____

Large

An elephant is a very large animal.

Write the word <u>large</u>.

_____

_____

A tractor is a big machine.

Write the word <u>big</u>.

_____

_____

Use this space to draw something that is big or large.

Name_____

Little

These pictures show things that are little.

Another word for little is small.

Draw a circle around the little bird.

Make a box around the small bug.

Can you put the little fish inside a big bubble?

Color all the other small things.

Name_____

Small

See the tiny little mouse.

Write the word <u>little</u>.

_____

- -

_____

This baby chicken is small.

Write the word <u>small</u>.

_____

- -

_____

See how many little or small things you can draw in the space below.

Name_____

Which is Which?

Color the smaller butterfly yellow.

Color the larger butterfly blue.

Which fish is smaller?
Make it blow bubbles.

Color the larger fish orange.

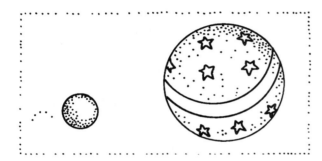

Which ball is smaller?

Color it green.

Color the larger one red.

Which flower is larger?

Put leaves on it.

Draw a bug on the smaller one.

Which umbrella is larger?

Make some raindrops falling on it.

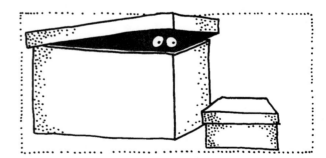

Color the smaller box blue.

Color the larger box red.

Put an X on the smaller box.

Name_____

Faces

This face is large.

This face is larger.

This face is the largest.

Make a red nose on the largest face.

Color blue eyes on the smallest face.

Color orange hair on the face that is neither the largest nor the smallest.

Name_____

Small Creatures

This mouse is small.

This mouse is smaller.

This mouse is the smallest of all.

Color the smallest mouse yellow.

Which bug is the smallest? Color it green.

Which bee is the smallest? Color it orange and red.

Name_____

Circle and Color

Scratch the largest of each group with your fingernail.

Then put a big circle around it.

Make a square with your crayon around the smallest of each group.

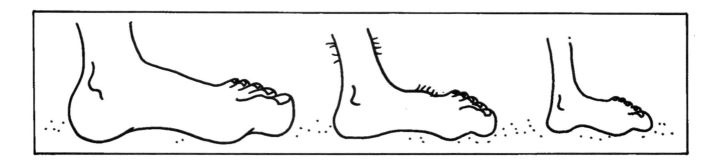

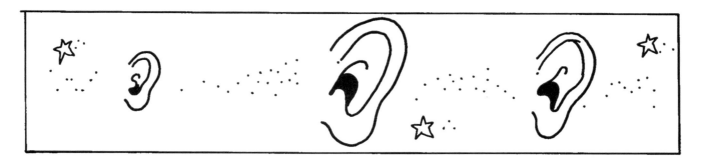

Name_____

Long and Short

A jump rope is long.　　　　A toothbrush is short.

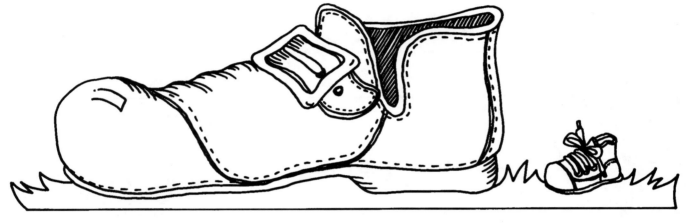

A giant's shoe is long.　　　　A baby's shoe is short.

A snake is long.　　　　An inchworm is very short.

Color the long things green.

Color the short things yellow.

Name_____

The Long and Short of It

Make a long red line in this box.

Make a short blue line in this box.

Which mouse has a long tail? Color him gray.

Which rabbit has short ears? Color them pink.

Which boy has a long nose? Draw a blue string around it.

Name_____

Long, Longer, Longest

The baby giraffe has a long neck.

The mother giraffe has a longer neck.

The father giraffe has the longest neck.

Which giraffe has the longest neck?

Put a leaf in its mouth.

Which giraffe has the shortest neck?

Draw a mouse on its back.

Name_____

Tall, Taller, Tallest

This ladder is tall.   This ladder is taller.   This ladder is the tallest.

Make your fingers walk up the tallest ladder and then write your name at the very top.

Make the shortest ladder reach a shelf with a cookie jar on it.

Use your yellow crayon to color the ladder that is neither the tallest nor the shortest.

Name_____

Mark the Road

The road to the lake is long.
The road to the bridge is longer.
The road to the airport is longest.

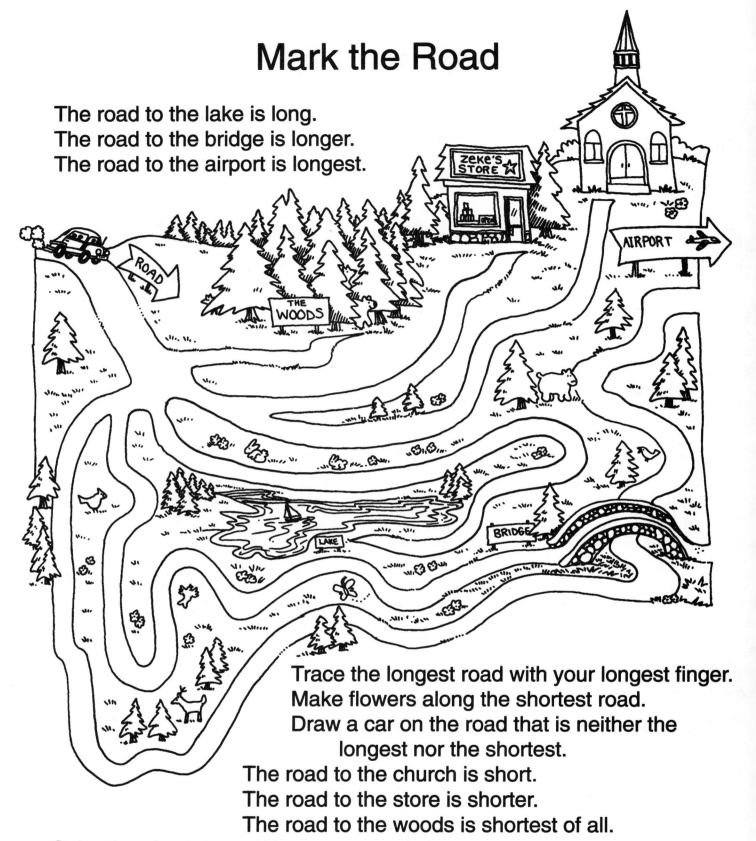

Trace the longest road with your longest finger.
Make flowers along the shortest road.
Draw a car on the road that is neither the longest nor the shortest.
The road to the church is short.
The road to the store is shorter.
The road to the woods is shortest of all.

Color the shortest road brown.
Make a purple line on the longest road.
Color grass along the road to the store.

Name_____

Fewer or More

Which hat has more feathers? Color that hat blue.

Which plate has fewer cookies? Color that plate yellow.

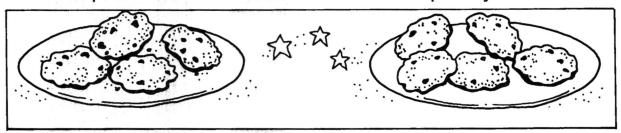

Which flower has fewer petals? Color it a pretty pink.

Which bunch has more balloons? Color it.

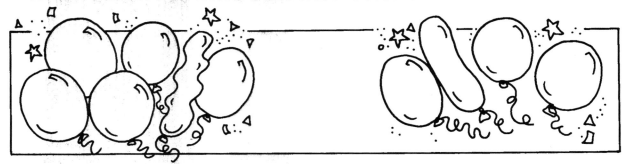

Name_____

Size Words Review

Fill the smallest jar with purple jelly.

Use your yellow crayon to light the tallest candle.

Put an X on the larger pair.

Catch the biggest bug in a circle.

Give the tallest flower leaves.

Draw a leaf for the smallest butterfly to rest on.

Make a sail for the shortest ship.

Name_____

Living With Numbers

Numbers . . . Numbers . . . Everywhere . . .

Numbers are a very important part of everyday life.

We need and use numbers for many reasons.

Look at all the ways we use numbers.

In this picture, circle every important number you can find.
Tell how or why each one is important.

Name_____

Special Numbers

Some numbers are special . . . just for you and your family.

The pictures below tell about these numbers.

Can you guess what they are?

If you live in a big city, your address might be on your house.

If you live in the country, your address might be on a mailbox like this one.

If you live in an apartment, your apartment number might be on a locked mailbox like these.

Write your address below.

Name_____

Telephone Time

Another special number is one that your friends use to call you on the telephone.

Each family or business has its own telephone number.

It is not the same as anyone else's telephone number.

Write your telephone number here.

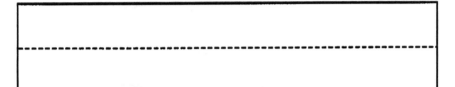

Make a pretend call to your house by pushing the correct buttons on this telephone.

Make another "fun" call to a good friend whose number you know.

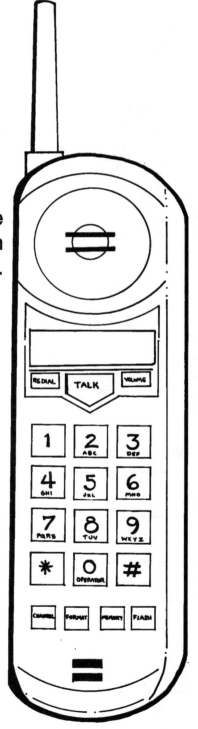

Name_____

Numbers with Buying Power

Most people of the world use money to buy things they need.

Around the world, money has many different names, but the paper money we use is called a <u>dollar</u>.

We use money to buy food and clothes and houses and toys.

There are many kinds of dollars. Each kind has different words and pictures, but most look something like this:

Write the word <u>dollar</u>.

Name_____

Dollar Bills

This is the mark or sign that says dollar.
It looks like the letter S with a straight line through it.

Make some dollar signs in this box.

If you bought a toy at the store, it might cost five dollars.

We write five dollars like this: **$5**

$5 is the price of the toy below. That is how much you must pay to buy the toy.

Write the price of the toy on its tag.

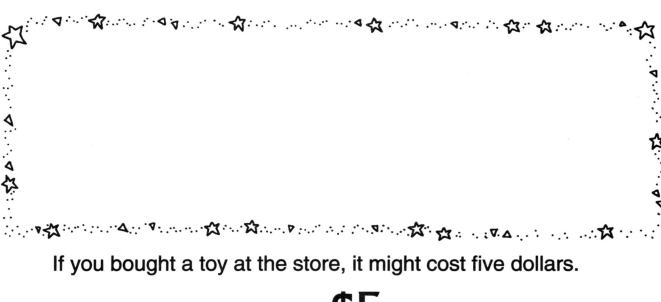

Write the words for its price.

Name_____

Toy Store

Each toy on this page has a price tag. It tells how many dollars you will need to buy the toy.

Circle the words that tell the correct price of each toy.

Five dollars
Three dollars
Two dollars

Six dollars
One dollar
Nine dollars

Two dollars
Three dollars
Eight dollars

Ten dollars
Six dollars
Seven dollars

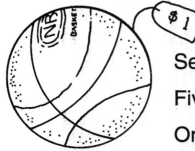

Seven dollars
Five dollars
One dollar

Four dollars
Five dollars
Nine dollars

Name_____

Price Tags

Pretend you are a salesperson in a clothing store. Your job is to write the correct price on each tag.

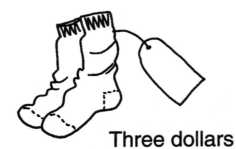
Three dollars

Six dollars

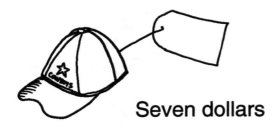
Seven dollars

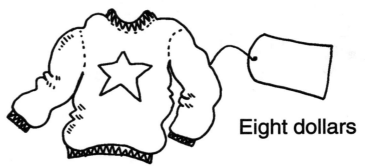
Eight dollars

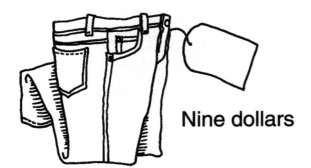
Nine dollars

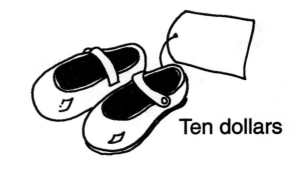
Ten dollars

Four dollars

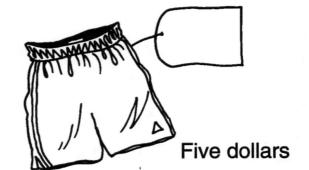
Five dollars

Name_____

Count and Rhyme

Write the numbers to finish this counting rhyme.

one, two

Buckle my 👞

_____

Shut the 🚪

_____

Pick up ✋

_____

Lay them straight

_____

A big, fat 🐔

Name_____

Numbers to Count Down!

Large rockets are used to lift spaceships high into space.

Before this happens, there is always a special countdown.

Help this spaceship lift off by doing the final countdown.

Write the numbers in the spaces.

10
9
___
___
___
___
___
___
___

IGNITION ...
BLAST OFF!

Name_____

The Race is On

These runners are in a big race. Can you tell who is winning?
Each runner is wearing a number.

Which runner is ahead? ____

Which runner is farthest behind? ____

Which runners are closest together? ____ and ____

Which runner is nearest a tree? ____

Which runner is nearest the lake? ____

Which runner do you think will win the race? ____

Name_____

Numbers to Grow On

Scales tell how heavy something is or how much it weighs.

Some scales measure in pounds.

Each mark on the scale stands for one pound.

This baby weighs eleven pounds.

The arrow points to the numeral 11.

The baby weighs _____ pounds.

Can you tell how much this kitten weighs?

It weighs _____ pounds.

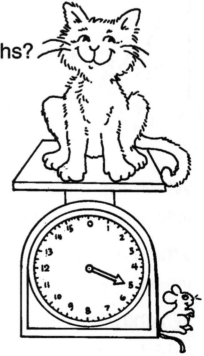

Use a scale to find out how much you weigh.

Write your weight here.

_____

Name_____

Weigh Up

Read the scales to tell how much each object below weighs.

____ pounds   ____ pounds   ____ pound

This child   These three books   This grown-up

weighs ____ pounds.   weigh ____ pounds.   weighs ____ pounds.

Name_____

All-New Creative Math Experiences

More Numbers to Grow On

To find out the size of things, we measure.

Rulers and measuring sticks tells us how long or tall things are.

Their marks tell us how many inches and feet or how many centimeters and meters an object is.

Inches

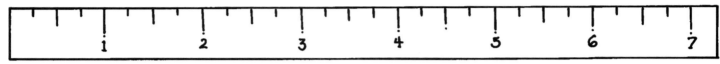

Centimeters

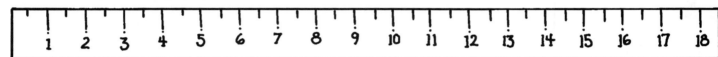

Which bookworm is the tallest? Color it green.

Put a red cap on the shortest one.

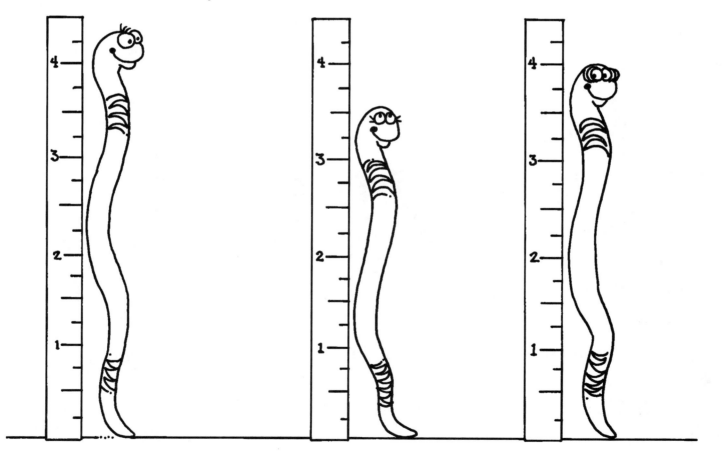

Name_____

Before there were measuring sticks, people used whatever they had handy to measure things. Usually, they used

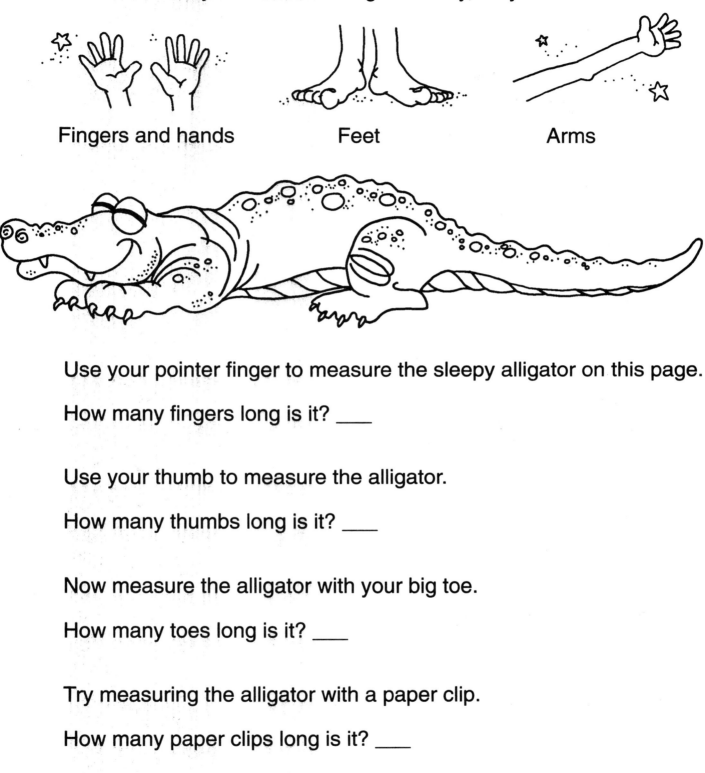

Fingers and hands   Feet   Arms

Use your pointer finger to measure the sleepy alligator on this page.

How many fingers long is it? ___

Use your thumb to measure the alligator.

How many thumbs long is it? ___

Now measure the alligator with your big toe.

How many toes long is it? ___

Try measuring the alligator with a paper clip.

How many paper clips long is it? ___

Why do you suppose people had to invent measuring sticks?

Name_____

Numbers for Travel

City streets often have number names.

Help Sandy choose the proper streets to get his errands done.

Which street should Sandy follow?

To get to the ball game he should take _____ Street.

To buy some sweets he should take _____ Street.

To get a tire fixed he should take _____ Street.

To visit his friend Hans Garcia, he should take _____ Street.

To go swimming he should take _____ Street.

Name_____

Mark the Trail

Very long, important highways or roads usually have numbers instead of names. Maps tell the number of each highway.

Betty gave Donald these directions to get from his house to her house. Mark the trail with a brown crayon to help Donald get there.

Dear Donald,
Take Hwy. 10 to Hwy. 405.
Stay on Hwy. 405 to Hwy. 101.
Take Hwy. 101 to Hwy. 75.
Take Hwy. 75 to my house.
Love, Betty

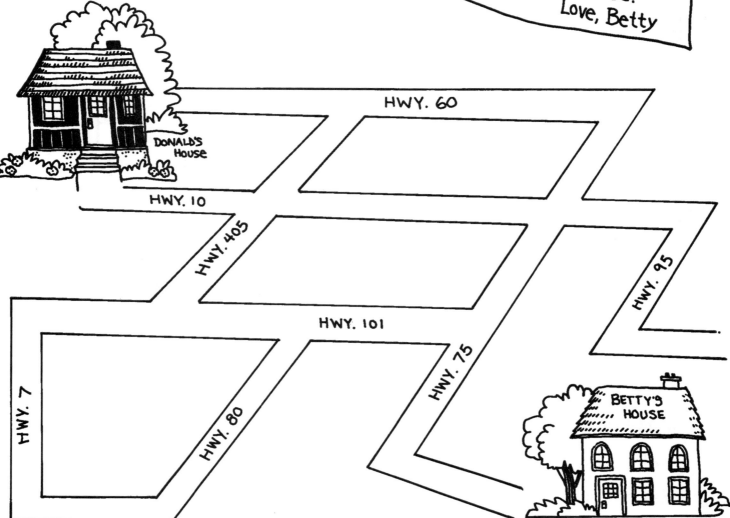

Name_____

Numbers to Celebrate

Calendars help us to remember the months and days of the year.

This is a page from a calendar. It is for the month of June. Each number on the calendar stands for a **day**.

How many days are there in June? _____

How many Sundays are there? _____

Make an X on the first day of June. Circle the last day.

Make a bright sun on a Wednesday.

Make a blue cloud for a rainy Monday.

Color each Saturday a different, happy color.

Name_____

Happy Birthday

Sunday	Monday	Tuesday	Wednesday	Thursday	Friday	Saturday

Make a calendar page for your birthday month.
   Color the space that shows your birthday a happy color.

What day of the week is your birthday this year? _____

Write the date of your birthday:

   Name of month _____

   Number of the day _____

Name_____

Numbers to Get Up and Go By

A clock tells us what time it is.

Clocks help us know when to get up, when to go to school, when to eat, and when to sleep.

The clock above shows one o'clock.

Circle the 1.

This clock shows three o'clock.

Circle the short hand that points to the number that tells the hour.

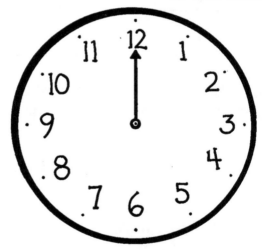

Make the short hand point to any hour you choose.

What time does the clock show? _____

Write it.

_____

Name_____

All-New Creative Math Experiences

What Time Is It?

_____ o'clock   _____ o'clock

_____ o'clock   _____ o'clock

Make this clock show the time to get up in the morning.   Make this clock show the time for lunch.

Name_____

This Is Buzzy

The pictures tell you what time Buzzy does things.

Can you make the short hour hand on each clock tell the correct time?

Buzzy gets up at seven o'clock.

Buzzy eats breakfast at eight o'clock.

Buzzy goes to school at nine o'clock.

Buzzy plays ball at three o'clock.

Buzzy takes a bath at six o'clock.

Buzzy is fast asleep at ten o'clock!

Name_____

Numbers for Finding Things

Pretend you are a delivery person. You must deliver packages and flowers to several people in a large apartment building.

Use the directory below to find the floor where each person lives.

"Touch" that button on the elevator with the correct color crayon.

Directory

Ms. Orange ....4th floor

Mr. Gray ....7th floor

Mr. Green ....8th floor

Ms. Brown ....6th floor

Ms. Black ....2nd floor

Ms. Blue ....5th floor

Mr. Yellow ....3rd floor

Ms. Red ....10th floor

Name_____

Numbers to Order and Eat

Numbers make it easy to order from some restaurant menus.

Menus tell the cost of each item.

MENU

1. Salad Delight $1.25
2. Soup-errific! $1.00
3. Diet Double $2.00
4. Chicken Lickin' $3.25
5. Hamburger Heaven $2.75
6. Hey, Hot Dog! $1.75
7. Rah! Rah! Ribs $4.50
8. Tea .... $.75
9. Milk .... $.60
10. Coffee .... $.75
11. Soda .... $.65
12. Ice Cream .... $.50 a scoop

What item number would you order if . . .

You loved chicken? .... _____

Your favorite meal was hot dogs? .... _____

You were on a diet? .... _____

You were a salad lover? .... _____

You wanted to spend exactly $1.00? .... _____

Name_____

Calorie Counting

People who are very careful about their health and body fitness often use numbers to help them choose the right foods.
They count the calories each food has.

Choose three of your favorite snacks from this list.
Write the names below and tell how many calories are in each.

- 1 peanut butter sandwich 225
- 1 small banana 81
- 1 medium apple 80
- 1 hard-boiled egg 81
- 1 large dill pickle 15
- $\frac{1}{2}$ cup raspberries 41
- 1 cucumber 29
- 1 chocolate bar 150
- 1 cup watermelon 42
- 10 pretzel sticks 12
- 7 fresh shrimp 70
- 1 cup cherries 65
- 1 cup puffed rice 55
- 5 crackers 60
- $\frac{1}{2}$ cup cantaloupe 24

My Favorite Snacks

	Snack	Calories
1.	_____	_____
2.	_____	_____
3.	_____	_____

Which snack has the fewest calories? _____

Which has the most? _____

Name _____

Measuring Cups

Sometimes we measure things in spoons and cups and bottles.

This cup will measure one cup of water.

One cup

This cup will measure one-half cup of water.

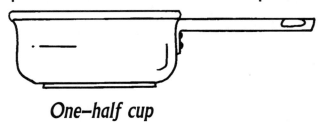

One–half cup

This cup will measure one-fourth cup of water.

One–fourth cup

It takes _____ half cups to make one full cup.

It takes _____ fourth cups to fill one half cup.

How many fourth cups does it take to fill one full cup? _____

Name_____

Measuring Up

These are measuring spoons.

$\frac{1}{4}$ teaspoon

$\frac{1}{2}$ teaspoon

1 teaspoon

1 tablespoon

Cooks use measuring spoons to measure ingredients for cooking.

CINNAMON TOAST
- Mix in a bowl:
    4 Tablespoons sugar
    ½ teaspoon cinnamon
- Make toast.
- Butter it.
- Sprinkle the cinnamon-sugar mixture on the toast.

CHOCOLATE MILK
1 cup milk

.... tablespoons of chocolate syrup.
- Place both in a glass.
- Stir with a spoon.

Circle the measuring spoons you would use to make this recipe.

Finish this recipe for chocolate milk.

Name_____

Whole and Half

This is
one whole apple.

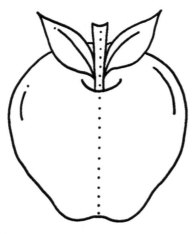

Trace the line to divide
the apple in half.

Now there are two
halves.

Each part is one half.

We write one half like this: $\frac{1}{2}$

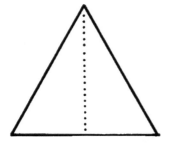 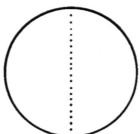 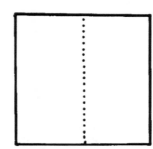 

Write $\frac{1}{2}$ on each half above.

When anything is divided in half, both halves must be the same size.

Name_____

Two Halves = One Whole

When two halves of something are put together, they make one **whole**.

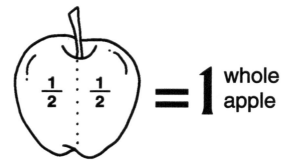

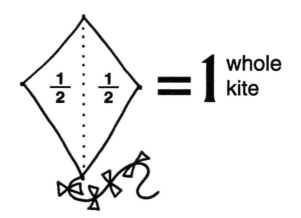

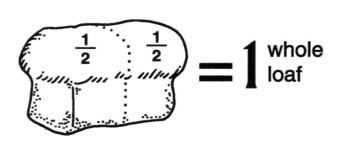

Draw a line to divide each shape in half.

Now draw a half to make each shape whole again.

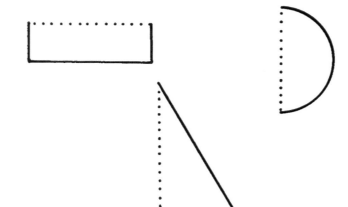

Write $\frac{1}{2}$ on each part.

Name_____

To make one half, you must cut exactly in the middle, so that both parts are exactly the same size.

If the shape below is divided in half, write **yes**.

If the shape is not divided in half, write **no**.

Half or Whole

Write the word <u>half</u> under each picture that shows one half.

Write the word <u>whole</u> under each picture that shows a whole.

Name_____

Hot and Cold

A thermometer has numbers that tell us how hot or cold something is. We say it tells us the temperature.

Read these thermometers and write the correct temperature beside each one.

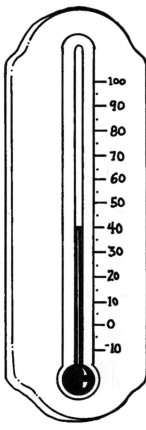

The thermometer outside the window tells the temperature of the air.

The temperature shown on this thermometer is _____ degrees.

A fever thermometer tells the temperature inside your body.

The temperature shown on this thermometer is _____ degrees.

Name_____

Check the Temperature

Which patient has the warmer body? Draw an ice pack on his or her head.

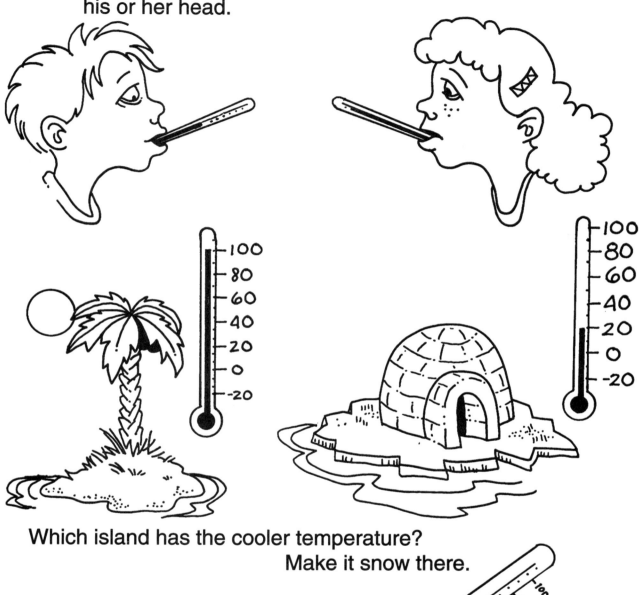

Which island has the cooler temperature?
Make it snow there.

This thermometer says it is cold.

The temperature is _____.

Name_____

Numbers on the Computer

This is a computer.

Numbers are important to computers.

There are hundreds of kinds of computers.
    Most of them need numbers to help them do their work.

This computer is programmed to tell about you. Make it tell your story.

Name _____

Address _____

_____

Height _____   Weight _____

Age _____   Date of birth _____

Number of brothers _____   Number of sisters _____

Number of Pets _____   Phone Number _____

Number of teeth lost so far _____

Name_____

Test Yourself

X Marks the Answer

Which is shorter?

Which is shortest?

Which is larger?

Which has the fewest feet?

$4 or $7. Which is greater?

Which is a pair?

Name_____

Circle the Set

     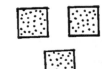

Circle the set of four.

Circle the greater set.

Circle two sets that are the same.

Circle the set with the fewest.

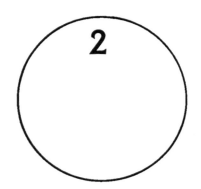 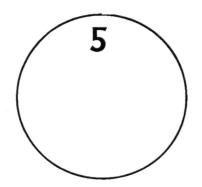 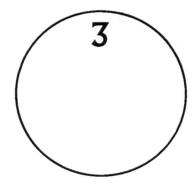

Draw a set to show the numeral in each circle.

Name_____

Which is Which?

Which picture shows something that measures hot and cold?
   Draw a squiggly line around it.

Which will tell you the day of the week? Color it yellow.

Which tells the hour? Make a mouse sitting on it.

Which can you use to buy something?
   Write its name under the picture.

Which measures the cinnamon you will need to make toast?
   Color it brown.

Which stores liquid for drinks? Fill it with yellow lemonade.

Name_____

Living With Numbers Review

Color three.	
Color $4.	
Color the set of six.	
Color the things that measure.	
Color the sign that shows the most miles.	
Color the halves.	
Color five o'clock.	

Name_____

Vocabulary for Math

Shapes	Four
Circle	Five
Square	Six
Triangle	Seven
Rectangle	Eight
Around	Nine
Number	Ten
Numeral	Zero
One	Many
Two	Sets
Three	Group

Name_____

Vocabulary for Math (cont.)

Pair	Shorter
Big	Shortest
Bigger	Long
Biggest	Longer
Large	Longest
Larger	More
Largest	Few
Little	Fewer
Small	Fewest
Smaller	Tall
Smallest	Taller
Short	Tallest

Name_____

Vocabulary for Math (cont.)

Size	Calendar
Telephone	Clock
Address	Time
Money	Cup
Dollar	Spoon
Price	One half
Count	One fourth
Scale	Thermometer
Weight	Temperature
Measure	Computer
Inch	Menu
Centimeter	

Name_____